CHARLIE and ALICE

A Friend in Need

Written by Deborah Abela
Illustrated by Stefano Tambellini

Published by Pearson Education Limited, Edinburgh Gate, Harlow, Essex, CM20 2JE
Registered company number: 872828

www.pearsonschools.co.uk

Original illustrations © Pearson Education, 2012
Illustrated by Stefano Tambellini
Cover design by Bigtop

First published 2012

2024
12

British Library Cataloguing in Publication Data
A catalogue record for this book is available from the British Library

ISBN 978 0 435 07598 9

Printed and bound by Great Britain by Ashford Colour Press Ltd.

Acknowledgements
We would like to thank the children and teachers of Bangor Central Integrated Primary School, NI; Barley Hill School, Thame; Bishop Henderson C of E Primary School, Somerset; Brookside Community Primary School, Somerset; Catcott Primary School, Somerset; Cheddington Combined School, Buckinghamshire; Cofton Primary School, Birmingham; Dair House Independent School, Buckinghamshire; Deal Parochial School, Kent; Holy Trinity Catholic Primary School, Chipping Norton; Lawthorn Primary School, North Ayrshire; Newbold Riverside Primary School, Rugby and Windmill Primary School, Oxford for their invaluable help in the development and trialling of the Bug Club resources.

Every effort has been made to contact copyright holders of material reproduced in this book. Any omissions will be rectified in subsequent printings if notice is given to the publisher.

Contents

Chapter 1
A Sneaky Surprise

"Come on, Charlie, it's not far now."

Alice White held her friend's hand and led him over the tussocky field of her grandma's farm. Charlie had a blindfold tied over his eyes and no idea where they were going.

"Watch that rock," Alice warned.

"Ouch!" Charlie stubbed his toe. "You mean the rock I just trod on?"

"Yes, that one." Alice giggled. "Don't worry, we're nearly there."

"If I make it," Charlie sighed. "Alice, please tell me where we're going."

"If I tell you, I'll be risking the safety of the entire world."

"The safety of the entire world?"

"If we're lucky!"

"Okay," said Charlie. "What have you done with the real Alice? The one who used to make sense?"

"Here we are," Alice announced.

"Here where?"

"Have a look."

Charlie lifted the blindfold from his eyes and pushed open the door to a barn.

"Surprise!" Charlie's foster parents, the Camilleris, and Alice's grandma greeted him with whistling and clapping. They were wearing party hats and standing around a table covered with roast chicken, potatoes and a steaming jug of gravy. In the centre was Alice's grandma's special chocolate cake with whipped cream and fresh strawberries. There were streamers, balloons and a large banner strung from one side of the barn to the other that said, 'Happy Birthday Charlie'.

"Is this all for me?" he asked quietly.

"It is unless you know another Charlie having a birthday today. Come on." Alice grabbed his hand. "They've spent hours getting this ready so we'd better not let it go cold."

Chapter 2
A Special Present

Mrs and Mr Camilleri served up the roast chicken and potatoes and poured out lashings of gravy.

"How come I didn't know about this?" Charlie asked.

"Because Alice did a very good job of keeping you out of the way while we got ready," Mrs Camilleri replied.

"I thought she was spending so much time with me because she liked my company."

"I do," Alice said between mouthfuls. "But I also love surprises and can be quite sneaky when I want to be."

Mr Camilleri clinked his spoon against his glass. "If I could have your attention everyone, we'd like to make a speech." He and Mrs Camilleri stood up.

"Thank you all for coming to this very special feast in honour of Charlie Fisher's birthday."

Alice and her grandma applauded and cheered.

"It's been a pleasure sharing our home with you, Charlie," Mrs Camilleri said. "You've brightened up the place and even though we only met a few months ago, it feels as if we've known you all our lives." She raised a glass of orange juice in the air. "To Charlie."

Everyone joined in.

"To Charlie."

"It's time for cake," said Grandma. She lit the candles and led a very loud version of Happy Birthday before adding, "Now it's time to make a wish." Charlie closed his eyes and was quiet for a few moments before he blew out the candles. A loud cheer filled the barn. Grandma began cutting the cake and handing out large slices.

Alice whisked a present from beneath the table. "This is for you."

Charlie undid the wrapping to find a set of writing paper and envelopes. "It's so you can write to your mum as often as you like."

"Thanks ..." Charlie's mouth clamped shut.

"Have you heard from her?" asked Alice.

Charlie shrugged. "Birthdays were never really a big deal at home."

"I'm sure she's thinking of you."

Charlie looked through his fringe. "Thanks."

Chapter 3
An Early Morning Visitor

Alice woke to a tap against her bedroom window. She threw off her blankets and swung aside the curtain. Charlie was in the garden waving a letter over his head. Alice frowned and opened the window.

"What are you doing?" she asked.

"I need you to come down. I have to show you something."

"Can't it wait until I'm up?" Alice rubbed her eyes.

"You are up," Charlie said, smiling. "I've already been waiting for an hour. If you're not careful you're going to sleep the day away."

Alice looked at the clock on her bedside table. "It's only seven o'clock. This had better be good, Charlie Fisher."

"It is." Charlie's smile stretched across his face. "It's the best."

Chapter 4
Big News

Charlie was pacing up and down in the kitchen when Alice came trudging down the stairs.

"I got a letter from my mum," he said.

Alice smiled. "Did she send you a birthday card?"

Charlie shook his head. "No. It's better than that. Look!" He held the letter as if it was the most precious thing he owned.

Alice read it out loud.

Dear Charlie,

Thank you for your letter! I hope life is treating you well. I have found a new flat. It's in a building that looks like a tall grey naval ship, but with little square portholes, that looks over a park near the river. It's small but big enough for the two of us and isn't far from the shop where we used to buy those chocolate milkshakes you liked. I've chatted to the owner about a job one evening a week. It won't be much but it will be enough to make a new start. Don't you think, Charlie?

Love, Mum

"See?" Charlie asked. "She's ready for me to come back."

Alice frowned. "Where does it say that?"

Charlie took the letter back and carefully folded it into his pocket. "Where she talks about a new start and finding a flat and a job ..."

"She's only *asked* about a job," Alice said carefully.

"She'll get it. My mum's a real charmer. The owner would be silly not to give it to her." Charlie paused. "I'm going back, Alice."

"When?"

"Now."

"*Now?* Do the Camilleris know?"

Charlie shook his head. "They know about Mum's letter but I didn't want to upset them by telling them I was going back."

"But you can't just *go!*" Alice pleaded. "What about the foster care people who brought you here? They need to know about this."

"They'll be okay, once they hear how well Mum's doing."

"Why don't we call her first, to make sure she's ready for you?"

"I don't know her 'phone number," Charlie replied.

"You don't have her address either, so how will you find her?"

"I'll buy a map of the city. I know the shop Mum wrote about, so I just need to look for the flats and the park near the river. And I've got a photo of her – I can ask if anyone knows where she is."

Alice felt her lip quiver. "But what about me?"

"We both have to go home one day," Charlie said quietly. "You to your parents when your brother's out of hospital, and me back to Mum. Now she's getting everything in place, I need to help her keep it that way. Don't worry though. Even if we lived on opposite sides of the world, we'd still be friends, I promise."

"At least stay until Grandma comes back from collecting the eggs. She'll be upset if you leave without saying goodbye."

"Sorry, Alice. I have to go. Thank you for everything and for being the best friend I ever had."

Then, just like that, Charlie was gone. He picked up his rucksack from where he'd left it by the fence and walked down the path away from Alice.

Chapter 5
An Important Decision

Alice ran to the edge of the garden, climbed onto the wooden fence for a better view, and searched the farm. If her grandma were here, she could talk Charlie into staying, but Alice couldn't see her anywhere. When she turned back she saw Charlie getting smaller as he walked further away.

Alice dashed back to the house and quickly pulled on some boots and a warm coat. In the kitchen, she threw some bread, cheese and an apple into her rucksack before scribbling a hurried note.

Dear Grandma,

Charlie and I have gone on a picnic.

Won't be home for lunch.

Love Alice xo

Alice ran out of the kitchen, slamming the door behind her. Her boots pounded on the ground as she desperately tried to see Charlie. It wasn't until she was at the end of Grandma's road that she could make out a shape walking between the hedgerows towards the ferry terminal.

"Charlie!" The wind carried her voice away.

There was a ferry waiting at the dock. It would be the last one for hours. She had to get down there. She had to reach Charlie.

Alice ran across the field. Her heart raced and her throat stung with the cold wind from the sea.

The ferry's horn blasted. It was about to leave.

She reached the terminal and slammed some money onto the ticket counter. "One return, please," she panted.

"You'll have to hurry!" The woman counted out Alice's change and handed over the ticket.

The ferry master unwound the coiled rope that held the ferry in place.

"Wait!" Alice bounded along the wharf and onto the gangplank. She took huge, sweeping breaths as she rushed onto the ferry.

There, on the front seat inside, with his chin resting on his knees, was Charlie.

"Can I sit down?"

"Alice?" Charlie dropped his legs to the floor. "What are you doing here?"

"I can't let you go to the city on your own," she said as she sat down beside him. "It's a big place and I've seen your muscles. They won't save you if you get into trouble!"

Charlie smiled. "Thanks, Alice."

"You're welcome," she grinned, snuggling in closer. "So, where exactly are we going?"

Chapter 6
A Long Wait

Charlie held the map up in front of him. "Let's try here," he said, pointing to a park near the river. "The shop Mum was talking about is nearby."

After the ferry crossing, they took a train to the city. The station escalators delivered them onto a busy street, with people rushing, cars honking and buses picking up and releasing hordes of passengers.

Charlie led the way off the main road into a series of side streets and alleys, shadowed by tall buildings and shopfronts, some with boarded and broken windows.

After passing the shop his mum had
mentioned in her letter, Charlie stopped
and looked around. On one side of them
lay a park; on the other, a towering, grey
building with small square windows. There
was rubbish by the entrance and the walls
either side were sprayed with graffiti.

"I think this is it." Charlie took a deep breath and, for a moment, he didn't move. "Where we lived before was much cleaner."

"I'm sure it's better inside," Alice said. "Let's go and find your mum."

A row of post boxes lined one of the hallway walls. Charlie found his mum's name on one of them, but no flat number.

"We'll have to ask someone," said Alice.

A group of kids pushed past them on the stairs. "Watch it!" one of them yelled as he ran into Charlie and burst out laughing.

They stopped in front of a door. Charlie wiped his hand against his jeans and knocked. They waited but there was no answer. He knocked on another door, but still nothing. A cold wind swept up from the ground floor. Charlie began to shiver.

They sat down on the floor and huddled together.

"We'll need to keep warm while we wait for someone to ask," Alice smiled.

Chapter 7
A Warning

"How's your little brother?" Charlie asked.

"Mum said he's getting better, but the doctors want to keep him in hospital for a bit longer."

"Do you miss them?"

"Yeah, but for now I'll have to make do with you." Alice nudged him in the side.

Charlie laughed. "Lucky for you I'm so charming then."

"So you keep telling me."

Charlie's smile melted away. "At least with family you're never lonely and there's always someone looking out for you. The Camilleris are really nice. They don't pretend to be my real mum and dad, but they're pretty close."

Footsteps echoed up the stairs.

"Someone's coming!" said Charlie.

A woman carrying a shopping bag walked towards them. She stopped and smiled at Charlie and Alice. "It's a bit cold to be sitting in the corridor, isn't it?"

"We're trying to find someone," Alice replied, showing her the photo of Charlie's mum. "Do you know her?"

The woman's face hardened. "Yes, I know her. She lives at number 8, and when you see her, tell her she still owes me that week's rent I lent her." She scrabbled for her keys, opened a nearby door, and slammed it behind her.

Charlie and Alice leaped to their feet and ran down the corridor to number 8. Charlie knocked quietly, but there was no answer.

"Try again," said Alice.

The door opened a fraction and a familiar face appeared. Charlie was about to call out, but his mum put a finger to her lips. Silently, she gave Charlie a big hug before ushering them inside. They heard the neighbour's door open briefly, before thudding shut.

Chapter 8
The Reunion

"It's so lovely to see you," Charlie's mum said as she pushed magazines from the table and put some mugs into an already crowded sink. "How did you find me?"

"I worked it out from your letter," Charlie said, "and we bought a map to make sure we didn't get lost."

"Aren't you clever?" His mum smiled and ruffled his hair. "I haven't been shopping yet so there's not much to offer you but how about a nice cup of tea?"

"I'll make it." Charlie grabbed the kettle and filled it. He opened the fridge. There was nothing apart from a shrivelled tomato and a carton of milk. He opened the carton and reeled from the sour smell.

"Sorry," his mum said. "I need to get some more."

"It doesn't matter," Alice said, reaching into her bag. "I've brought some bread, cheese and an apple."

"It'll be like having a picnic," Charlie's mum smiled.

Charlie grabbed a plate and cut up the apple and cheese.

"You must be Alice. Charlie told me about you in his letter," she smiled. "You're even prettier than he said."

Alice blushed.

"How are the people you're living with, Charlie? Are they treating you well?"

"They're really nice. They gave me my own room and they're great cooks. How are you, Mum? Did you get the job?"

"No," she shook her head. "It didn't … work out, but I'm sure I'll find something else."

Charlie looked at the frayed armchairs, the material pinned up as curtains, and the dirty mugs piled on the coffee table.

"It's different this time, Charlie. I can feel it. It won't be long now. Things are really going to change for me. Now, tell me about everything you've been up to."

Chapter 9
The Long Journey Home

Later that afternoon, Charlie's mum gave him a hug like she never wanted to let him go. She wiped away her tears and promised him they'd be together again soon, before quietly opening her front door. She shot a quick look at the neighbour's flat, then put her fingers to her lips. Charlie and Alice tiptoed away.

As they sat together on the train, Charlie stared out of the window in silence.

He still hadn't said a word when they climbed off the last ferry of the day. His footsteps were heavy and his body hunched down into his coat.

It was late and the sun was already falling behind the island's hills. Alice took her torch from her bag and lit up the path.

"One thing I like about living on the island is how many stars you can see. I know there are the same number as in the city, but it's like they come out especially for us," she said.

Charlie dug his hands deeper into his pockets.

"When I first came here," Alice said, "I thought I'd hate it on my own. My grandma said you and I would be good friends. I told her I had enough friends at home, but she was right. I've never had a friend like you."

Charlie sniffed into the darkness and
stopped walking. "She's always going to
be like that, isn't she?" he said. "I'm never
going to be able to go home."

Alice shrugged just a little. "You have to keep hoping you'll go home one day, but for now, the island is your home – with the Camilleris, Grandma and me."

She held out her arms. Charlie fell into her hug and after a deep breath, cried into her shoulder.

Chapter 10
Homecoming

It was dark when they reached Grandma's house. All the lights were on and there was a car parked on the drive.

"Mum's here!" Alice hurried inside, with Charlie close behind.

"Oh, thank goodness, you're back." Grandma swept them in for a hug, kissing each of them on the forehead. "Are you okay? Is everything all right?"

They both nodded.

Alice's mum offered no hug, just a stern look. "Where have you been? Do you know what time it is?"

Alice looked at the clock on the wall. It was later than she had thought. "I'm sorry."

"That's it?" her mother exploded. "You're *sorry*? You've been missing since this morning! I've driven the whole way out here and all you've got to say is 'sorry'?"

Alice stood still, not knowing what to do.

"I don't have time to go chasing after you, Alice. We have enough to worry about with your brother without *you* causing trouble."

"They're here now," Grandma said. "They're safe."

"*Now* they are," Alice's mum shot back. "You left a note saying you were going on a picnic."

"We needed to see someone." Alice sneaked a quick look at Charlie.

"Does this have something to do with you?" demanded Alice's mum.

Charlie nodded. "It was my idea. Alice tried to talk me out of it but I wouldn't listen."

"Where did you go?"

"To the city," Alice admitted.

"The city?" her mum shouted. "Do you know how dangerous it is to be roaming around the city on your own?"

"We had each other," Alice said.

"But you're just kids! You can't make decisions like that on your own. What were you thinking?"

Alice looked at Charlie. He seemed small, as if the day had worn him away and his voice was almost a whisper. "I just wanted to see my mum and make sure she was okay."

"Is she all right, Charlie?" Grandma asked.

Charlie nodded.

"It was still a very dangerous thing to do," cried Alice's mum. "I'm sorry about your mother but what if something had happened to my daughter? What if she'd been hurt?"

"You probably wouldn't have noticed," Alice snapped.

Her mum stopped, her eyes wide. "Excuse me?"

"You haven't paid attention to me for years, so why would you start now?"

Her mother pointed at Charlie. "Did you teach her to act like this? To be irresponsible and disrespectful? How ..."

"Stop yelling at Charlie. He's done nothing wrong," sobbed Alice.

"He made you follow him to the city."

"He didn't make me. I wanted to go because he needed a friend. You don't even notice me most of the time. You only ever think about Simon and how ill he is. You never even tell me the truth about him."

Her mother quietened. "Alice, I do, I …"

"No you don't. I don't know what's wrong with him or how serious it is. You say he has weak lungs and that everything will be okay but you don't *know* that. I'm old enough to know what's going on, or to help, but you keep treating me like a baby."

Alice was really crying now. "All Charlie wanted to do was see his mum. Why is that so wrong?"

Alice's mum shook her head. "It's not wrong, sweetie. It's a perfectly reasonable thing to want. I guess all mums can get things wrong sometimes."

Slowly, quietly, she raised her arms and Alice ran to her without a word.

"I'll call the Camilleris and tell them you're okay," Grandma said, giving Charlie another kiss. "They were so worried about you both. We all were."

Chapter 11
A Midnight Feast

To help her stay calm while Charlie was
missing, Mrs Camilleri had been cooking.
After Grandma called, the Camilleris
rushed over with lasagne, garlic bread, and
a giant sticky toffee pudding.

There were tears and hugs as Mrs and Mr Camilleri told Charlie how worried they had been about him and how relieved they were that he was safe and back with them.

It was up to Alice to remind them that they hadn't eaten since lunch.

"Of course!" The adults bustled around the kitchen bringing out knives and forks. Soon, their plates were filled with food.

Alice whispered to Charlie, "Looks like you were missed."

Charlie nodded, his face red and his eyes glistening. "Maybe you were right. Maybe I can have more than one home."

"Oh, I think you'll find I'm always right."
Alice helped herself to more lasagne.
"You're luckier than most of us who only
have one family, but I guess it's because of
all that charm of yours."

"Thank you, Alice."

"For finally admitting you are charming?"

"For bringing me home."

"You're welcome," Alice shrugged. "I've become used to having you around, Charlie Fisher, and I rather like it that way."